W9-AXB-800

HONG KONG

PACIFIC CENTURY PUBLISHERS LTD

Copyright © 2006 Pacific Century Publishers

All rights reserved. No part of this publication may be reproduced or transmitted in any form or by any means, electronic or mechanical, including photocopy, recording or any information storage and retrieval system, without permission from the publisher.

Photography by: Angela Wong 63 (bottom); Cathay Pacific 27 (middle); China Guides Series Ltd, 63 (second from top); C.T.H. Smith Images 16 (bottom); Greg Girard 5, 39 (top), 42 (top), 43 (left three), 51, 73 (top); HKRFU 44-45; Jacky Yip 34-35, 41 (top), 55, 56 (top), 63 (top left), 75 (top); Joan Law 10-11, 19 (top), 20, 39 (bottom left), 50 (top), 52, 54 (top), 58, 59, 77 (top); Kasyan Bartlett 1, 6-7, 12-13, 14 (first & third right), 22-23 (bottom), 24-25, 26 (top and bottom), 27 (top), 28-29 (top), 33 (top), 48, 49 (top), 60-61, 64-65, 66-67, 68, 69 (top); Keith Macgregor 14 (second & fourth right); 16 (top), 17, 18 (top), 21, 22 (top), 23 (top), 26 (both middle), 27 (bottom), 28 (bottom), 29 (bottom), 30-31 (bottom), 32, 33 (bottom), 36, 37, 38, 39 (bottom right), 40, 41 (bottom), 46-47, 49 (both bottom), 50 (bottom), 53 (both), 54 (bottom), 56 (bottom), 57 (all), 62, 63 (third left & right), 69 (bottom), 72 (all), 73 (bottom), 74, 76, 77 (bottom), 78-79, 80; Leong Kai Tai 43 (right); Li Suk Woon 70-71; Pat Lam 18 (bottom); Tony Yu 2-3, 8-9, 14 (left), 30-31 (top)

Cover photographs: Kasyan Bartlett & Tony Yu

Cover & back cover design: Marina Mok

Production: Ronna Lau

Published by Pacific Century Publications
Printed in Hong Kong

ISBN 988-98125-8-4

P1
Two International Finance Centre makes the rest of Hong Kong's skyscrapers look small by comparison. Completed in 2003, this building - the third tallest in Greater China - was designed by Cesar Pelli and is 88 storeys (an extremely lucky number in Chinese) high. It was designed to accommodate financial firms and the Hong Kong Monetary Authority is located on the 55th floor.

Known as Two ifc, the building's top floor is actually slightly higher than the city's landmark viewing gallery on the Peak. It should be noted too that, even though the top floor is the 88th, there are not actually 88 storeys. Some numbers like 14 and 24 are taboo in Cantonese and have been omitted.

P2-3
Thousands of lights from Hong Kong's skyscrapers twinkle at night to create its famous skyline. The tall building towards the right is the 88-storey Two International Finance Centre, while the Hong Kong Convention and Exhibition Centre is the stingray-shaped building jutting out into Victoria Harbour.

Right
While the activity in some parts of the territory ebbs away with the setting sun, Hong Kong's night markets are just getting started. Hawkers begin setting up shop around seven in the evening, offering everything from food to pirated cassettes or the latest in badly made copies of designer sportswear. Temple Street Market, close to Jordan MTR station, is one of the largest night markets with hundreds of stalls.

P6-7
The view towards Wanchai and Central districts on a clear sunny day. Up behind the business districts are the up-market residences on the Peak, with the wok-shaped viewing tower in the centre. Beyond Hong Kong itself you can see hills on the island of Lantau in the background.

P8-9
The rising sun reflects off the buildings on Hong Kong's famed waterfront as another day dawns on the city's financial district.

Pages 10–11
A Cantonese opera to placate marauding ghosts and charm the hearts of humans. Members of one of Hong Kong's two main fishing tribes, the Hoklo, perform during the Cheung Chau Bun Festival.

Pages 12-13
Tradition continues in Hong Kong in ways other than just festivals. Ancient farming methods are practised in fishponds such as these near Yuen Long in the New Territories, but are threatened by the constant demand for human habitation.

INTRODUCTION

Everything changes, much remains the same. After more than 150 years of British rule, Hong Kong has a new sovereign. But, the new is really old, China has reclaimed her own. The old colony has been transformed into a new Special Administrative Region (SAR); the face of the government is new, but the faces of the administration are largely unchanged. Contrasts and contradictions abound as Hong Kong reveals itself sometimes subtly, other times dramatically as the confluence of two cultures: Chinese and Western. The ancient rituals of geomancy stand side by side with soaring, hi-rise, hi-tech universal approaches to business and finance, the abacus with the Internet, Taoist and Buddhist temple with church, superstition with quality control, snake soup with fast food, the mobile telephone with herbal medicines, Cantonese with English and numerous other tongues, flags of convenience, rates of exchange, chopsticks and horse racing, calligraphy, neon and incense.

The realities of Hong Kong's geography have done much to shape these present-day characteristics. Situated on the southeast coast of China at the mouth of the Pearl River, 122 kilometres away from the trading centre of Guangzhou, the SAR comprises the island of Hong Kong; Kowloon, on the mainland opposite; and the New Territories to the north. Kowloon and the New Territories form a peninsula which borders the Shenzhen Special Economic Zone along the Shenzhen River from Deep Bay in the west to the northern shore of Mirs Bay in the east. The territory also includes more than 230 islands, the largest being Lantau, larger even than Hong Kong Island. The coastline is irregularly and often dramatically indented; hills rise spectacularly as high as 900 metres, leaving little room for agriculture, but a territory perfectly suited for shipping. The total area of Hong Kong is 1,091 square kilometres, making land an extremely valuable commodity.

Located just south of the Tropic of Cancer, Hong Kong has a subtropical climate. From May to October, the warm, moist southwest monsoon generally brings temperatures between 26 and 33 degrees Celsius and humidity often as high as 90 per cent. Most of the rain falls during this summer period and typhoons occasionally threaten normal day-to-day activities—an early warning system operates and if the typhoon comes too close everyone is advised to go home and stay indoors until it passes. From October to May, the weather is generally warm and dry with temperatures ranging from 14 to 28 degrees Celsius.

Hong Kong's first known inhabitants were the Hundred Yue, a maritime people who populated much of China's southeastern seaboard during the second millennium BC. Little is known about their living habits, language or ethnic origins, except for the intriguing clues left in the geometric-style rock carvings found at Shek Pik on Lantau Island, Kau Sai Chau, Po Toi, Cheung Chau and Tung Lung Islands, and at Big Wave Bay and Wong Chuk Hang on Hong Kong Island.

Coins found in Hong Kong suggest that the military conquest of south China by the northern powers during the Qin (221–207 BC) and Han (206 BC–220 AD) dynasties probably brought settlers into the area. In 1955, a fine brick-built tomb was uncovered at Lei Cheng Uk with an array of typical Han tomb furniture. It is the finest monument from the turbulent early to middle years of this period. Pottery and iron tools have also been found at Pak Mong on Lantau Island, on Kau Sai Chau Island and Tung Wan Tsai on Ma Wan Island, revealing the lives of a relatively sophisticated people.

Archaeological remains from later periods are surprisingly rare, although Tang dynasty (618–907 AD) dome-shaped lime kilns, which have been found on some local beaches, indicate that lime was a valuable commodity, probably used for protecting boats from salt water, dressing agricultural fields and as a building material.

Above
During the annual bun festival on the island of Cheung Chau, thousands of villagers and visitors crowd the narrow streets to watch a colourful procession where children like this young boy dressed in historical costume are paraded on concealed poles above head-height.

Below
On Hong Kong's outlying islands and in the villages of the New Territories, it is still possible to find women wearing traditional Hakka headgear.

Strong verbal traditions, nevertheless, link Hong Kong with the Mongol incursions into China, and the end of the Song dynasty in the 13th century. And recent excavations on Tung Lung Island have revealed details of an Imperial Chinese fortification, suggesting that some strategic importance was attached to the area. The former Kowloon Walled City was also the location of a military garrison during the Qing dynasty (1644–1911). Nevertheless, prior to the arrival of the British, the population was only about 3,650, living in 20 or 30 scattered villages, with an additional 2,000 fishermen living on boats.

The British had been trading in China since the opening of the eastern sea routes by the Portuguese in the 16th century. But, like all foreigners, their activities were strictly limited to seasonal trading at Canton (Guangzhou) by the local authorities who saw no use for western products. Attitudes on both sides were unhelpful. In September 1834, the Governor of Canton said, "The common disposition of the English barbarians is ferocious, and what they trust in are the strengths of their ships and their guns."

For their part, the British merchants were resentful of the controls imposed upon them. In December 1834, they presented a petition to London to remove the trade restrictions and challenge the 'arrogant assumption of supremacy' claimed by the Chinese. Most foreign merchants were engaged in the opium trade, which they called 'a harmless luxury'. They wanted to extend their dealings in China, not limit them.

With Canton proving increasingly unworkable, Captain Charles Elliott was instructed by Whitehall to find a 'conveniently situated' island with a harbour close enough to facilitate trade with China, but far enough away to avoid Chinese interference. The Bonin Islands, Hong Kong, Lantau and Formosa were all suggested as possibilities.

When Elliott's men raised the Union Jack at Possession Point on 26 January 1841, his superiors back in London were not impressed. British Foreign Secretary, Lord Palmerston, called the new colony 'a barren rock with hardly a house upon it.' But Britain now had a firm trading post close to China. Just a few months later the population was estimated to have increased to 15,000, and by 1847 to more than 23,800. But the figures tell only a part of the story: incessant comings and goings in the pursuit of trade, particularly between Hong Kong and China, were a prominent feature of daily life (as, of course, they still are today), making accurate estimates difficult.

True to the predictions of cynical London, Hong Kong was initially unable to compete with affluent, powerful Chinese cities like Canton and Shanghai. Free from mainland obstinacy and the British legal system, the new settlement became a magnet for the less principled of Queen Victoria's empire and Imperial China. For several years, early Hong Kong officials appear to have spent more time controlling its lawless residents, some of whom came from within the authorities' own ranks, than developing Hong Kong as a commercial centre. In 1847, for example, a public enquiry found JW Hulme guilty of habitual drunkenness and forced him to return to England—he was the Chief Justice.

Nevertheless, from the very start government policy was *laissez-faire* with limited taxation. Hong Kong was a marketplace open to all, as it is today, and where the government was supposed to be impartial and non-interfering. This partly explains official ambivalence towards the opium trade, although its prevalence and profitability also made it difficult to eradicate. Shortly after John Davis became governor in 1844, he said that, "almost every person possessed of capital who is not connected with government employment, is employed in the opium trade." This included the major *hongs*, or trading houses.

From the start of Samuel Bonham's governorship in March 1848 to the end of Hercules Robinson's in March 1865, tremendous economic growth took place in Hong Kong. In Bonham's first year in office, 700 ships totalling more than 228,000 tons entered and cleared Victoria Harbour; in the last year of Robinson's, the equivalent figures were almost 5,000 ships totalling more than 2,000,000 tons. Much of this boom in overseas trade was the result of Chinese emigration throughout Southeast Asia, Australia and North America.

During the overthrow of the Manchu Qing dynasty in 1911, many people made their way from China to Hong Kong, swelling the population to 486,000. A curious amalgam of cultures and ideas resulted: Chinese customs were practised alongside colonial attitudes and bullish commercialism. Three groups dominated: Europeans, compradores (the chief agents of the foreign business houses), and Chinese, who constituted the majority of the people. Above all Hong Kong was a place to make money, and traders from all over the world flocked to share in the spoils.

Despite its rapid growth in people and commerce, Hong Kong at this time was hardly at the centre of the modern world. There was no drinking water reservoir, no university and the governor moved around his domain in a sedan chair. A journey from Kowloon to the Peak was a major expedition involving three separate rickshaw rides as well as a trip on the Star Ferry across the harbour.

Prevailing attitudes and activities among the expatriate community were those of 'little England' with peculiar Hong Kong characteristics. The higher up the Peak your address, the higher up the social scale you were. The Establishment worked at Jardine, Swire, the Hong Kong Bank, and lunched sedately in the Hong Kong Club. Saturdays meant racing at Happy Valley, tea dances at Repulse Bay, and possibly a weekend bungalow at Shek O.

For the majority of Hong Kong people life was much less grand. Often they worked terrible hours for a pittance. Their living conditions, as British travel writer Henry Norman stated at the time, were 'probably about as insanitary as any place in the globe under civilised rule'. Yet educated and talented Chinese were already breaking with the traditions of Hong Kong's brief history, forming groups like the Tung Wah to pursue social reform, and, perhaps most importantly, to build business empires and accumulate private fortunes that would eventually lead to the modern Hong Kong economic miracle.

Men like Ng Choy, the first Chinese member of the Legislative Council, and Robert Ho Tung, Hong Kong's first millionaire, were willing to tolerate foreign rule, but they retained intact their heritage, culture and traditions, in effect safeguarding the essential 'Chineseness' of Hong Kong. The brief occupation of Hong Kong by the Japanese during World War II did little to alter the fact that this is and always has been a mainly Chinese territory. After several years of negotiation, Hong Kong returned to China as a Special Administrative Region on 1 July 1997 with a local chief executive rather than a British governor.

Today, Hong Kong is home to 6.5 million of some of the hardest-working people on earth—97 per cent are Chinese and extremely affluent by world standards. Per capita GDP is around US$24,500, which is higher than some EU member states. Life expectancy for men is 75 years, 81 years for women. Hong Kong is the world's eighth-largest trading economy; the third-busiest financial centre; the site of the world's busiest container port; the world's largest producer of timepieces; and, according to a recent survey, the world's freest economy. Office rents are among the world's highest, however, and therefore occasionally discourage businesses from setting up shop in Hong Kong.

Shipping is the territory's most obvious money earner: the procession of container ships through the East Lamma Channel to the Kwai Chung Container Port is never-ending. Ships arrive from every corner of the globe, carrying every product known to

Every ten years, the tiny island of Tap Mun holds a special version of an annual festival to placate evil spirits. Tap Mun's small population is joined by villagers from nearby island communities to enjoy perfomances of Cantonese opera by visiting puppeteers from Guang-dong province. Their colourful puppets depict characters from ancient Chinese folklore.

In traditional houses like the one above, tenants read or carry out household chores unperturbed by the lack of windows or the feeble light from an electric bulb. Below effigies of Buddhist and Taoist gods still stand guard in the SAR's more than 360 temples.

man, filling 14.5 million containers in 1997. Only a handful of their contents are destined for local consumption. Re-exports have led Hong Kong to be called a 'transformation economy'. This applies even to commodities like stocks, shares and money—just about everything is available for a price.

The highly lucrative and complex financial industries, myriad commercial and merchant banks and insurance companies occupy the highest profile office blocks in Central at exorbitant per-square-foot costs: Exchange Square, Jardine House, The Landmark, Citibank Tower, Worldwide House, Hutchison House, Bank of America Tower, Far East Finance Centre, Lippo Centre, Bank of China Tower, Citibank Plaza, Standard Chartered Bank Building, Alexandra House. Spin-off industries that support them thrive: design houses, advertising agencies, public relations companies, accountants, lawyers and 'consultants' are innumerable.

The old British-based *hongs*, which once controlled large sections of the early Hong Kong economy, no longer dominate as they once did. Swire, with its considerable retail property portfolio and large stake in Cathay Pacific Airways, Hong Kong's major airline, is, in many ways, a truly multinational company. Jardine's is much more anonymous, but just as ever-present—from the import of fine wines to property management. Known alternatively as 'Wayfoong, the Abundance of Remittances', 'The Bank', or more recently HSBC, the Hongkong and Shanghai Banking Corporation dominates the local market, and has developed its overseas activities and assets to make it one of the world's top ten banks. All three *hongs* are still major players, but many other local companies are now their equals.

Nowadays, the star performers in the Hong Kong business world are men like Li Ka Shing of Cheung Kong and Hutchison Whampoa, who have created vast business empires that spread into China, Southeast Asia and many other parts of the world. These are today's folklore heroes, who have built great personal fortunes on Hong Kong's most precious and limited resource—land. Their every move is intensely scrutinised by the local press, absorbed, consumed and analysed. There's a lot at stake.

Despite the incredible prices of flats, the acquisition of property is a passion in Hong Kong. When prestigious new developments go on sale, queues frequently form to earn the right to purchase the available apartments. A 700 square foot flat in a fashionable middle-class area may cost as much as HK$3,000,000—the equation is made even more mind-boggling by the fact that banks may lend as much as 70 per cent.

It probably explains why Hong Kong people work so hard. Officially the working week is 44 hours, but 70 hours a week is frequent. As a result, it is not uncommon for a person to have two or more jobs. A manager in a large office may simultaneously be running his own business. Flexibility and adaptability are at the heart of Hong Kong's economic success, and for many the rewards have been quite staggering.

Rolls-Royces, Mercedes Benzes, BMWs and Porsches are common sights on the city's crowded thoroughfares. Designer fashion is standard attire. Rolex, Cartier and Breitling are the watch brands of choice.

Hong Kong parades its affluence conspicuously, boldly, elegantly on the wrist, feet, shoulders. The best is available across the city in department stores like Seibu, Sogo, Mitsukoshi, Lane Crawford, Wing On and Sincere. But the Landmark and Prince's Building in Central, Pacific Place in Admiralty, Harbour City in Tsim Sha Tsui and Times Square in Causeway Bay are the premier centres for chic fashion, accessories, jewellery, perfume and cosmetics. The names of the international design elite are household names: Alfred Dunhill, Gianni Versace, Giorgio Armani, Christian Dior, Lanvin, Hugo Boss, DKNY.

Fabulous jewellery of gold, diamonds, opals, pearls and auspicious jade, which local people believe protects the wearer, make Hong Kong a veritable Aladdin's cave of treasure. Specialist designs can be made according to taste, or more classic items like finely-wrought gold chains or gem-encrusted necklaces selected from a vast array of shops. The honourable doors of traditional merchants like King Fook, Tse Sui Luen and Emperor are watchfully guarded at gunpoint throughout the main shopping areas: contemporary local jewellery designer talent like Kai-yin Lo stand crown-to-crown with esteemed foreign purveyors such as Bulgari and Chopard.

Audio and video, computers, cameras and photographic equipment shops are numerous—not surprising for a city where technology is not a toy, but a potential tool for advancement. In Causeway Bay and along Tsim Sha Tsui's Nathan Road retail outlets appear to offer every conceivable device by Sony, Panasonic, Kenwood, Technics, Apple, Minolta and the rest. Minidisc players, video cameras, multi-system VCRs, karaoke machines and televisions, notebooks, modems, auto-focus cameras and accessories are but the tip of the iceberg in this technology-mad city.

Hong Kong's reputation as the R&R venue for the military off duty was well-deserved until the 1970s. These days there is much more variety. Thousands of Chinese, Asian and international restaurants, many of world-class standard; bars and nightclubs make the city one of the world's hottest party spots. There is classical and modern, Western and Chinese theatre, music, ballet and opera; multi-screen cinemas with international and local films showing; horse racing at Happy Valley and Shatin (Hong Kong people are the world's biggest gamblers).

Lan Kwai Fong is the Central business district's playground. Here the multinational young and lovely interface with the braces and striped shirts of high finance outside trendy bars like California and Club 97. At street level and above, contemporary restaurants with designer menus provide fashionably romantic dinners at tastefully arranged prices.

Nearby, the Fringe Club is Hong Kong's main alternative venue for theatre, music and exhibitions, where Harold Pinter meets with the local dance troupe Zuni Icosahedron. More mainstream at City Hall in Central, Chopin, Mozart and Beethoven are performed regularly by the Hong Kong Philharmonic and visiting international orchestras and soloists. But the strains of the Pearl River symphony are just as likely to be heard as those of Beethoven's Ninth.

Pulsating Wanchai is much less esoteric. Lockhart Road with its girly bars, saunas and massage parlours still appeals to some, though unsuspecting visitors might consider leaving their credit cards in the hotel before stepping through the red velvet curtains. But the main attractions are the non-stop party venues like Joe Banana's, the China Jump and JJ's. The music is loud, 'in-your-face', the temperature hot and the people irrepressible. In Wanchai, it doesn't matter where you come from just as long as you like staying out late.

Across the neon-flooded harbour in Tsim Sha Tsui, the more traditional, cognac-savouring, Chinese trading community works at leisure: hostess bars, karaoke bars, hotels with floor shows and live music abound with flashing gold, signature Rolexes and mobile telephones. Club Bboss, the area's best known night spot with its army of seductive hostesses, at one time considered going public, placing its shares on the Hong Kong stock market.

Traditional Chinese style and practices permeate Hong Kong life. Taoist art is still abundant and herbal tea is essential to many, but the venerable architecture has mostly disappeared.

Close by, the Hong Kong Cultural Centre, the territory's premier performing arts venue, is home to a different body of work. Consummate productions of *Les Miserables*, *Cats*, *Phantom of the Opera*, *Flying Dutchman* and *Barber of Seville* are just a few of the many major events showcased in recent years in its state-of-the-art auditoria. Along the

Above
A Yi Wu player rehearses for a performance during a Taoist festival; a man finds another use for a temple besides worshipping; and villagers of a walled city cluster at its gateway decorated in honour of the birthday of To Tei Kung, the earth god.

Right
Neon reflections in the harbour echo the rocket-like towers of Hong Kong island dominating the urban sprawl of the Kowloon peninsula.

Tsim Sha Tsui waterfront, next door to the Hung Hom KCR station, stands the mammoth, 10,000-seater Coliseum. Local Canto-pop stars like Leon Lai and Aaron Kwok play to full houses for weeks at a time. Western rock legends like Sting, Eric Clapton, Elton John and Paul Simon have also packed it to the rafters, if only, modestly, for one or two nights.

The prevalence of Chinese traditions alongside western ideas is also seen in Hong Kong's acknowledgment of two calendars. Gazetted public holidays are drawn from both the international solar and Chinese lunar calendars: Christmas, New Year and Easter, Chinese New Year, Ching Ming and Mid-Autumn Festival are all celebrated in Hong Kong.

Chinese New Year is the most important holiday on the lunar calendar, falling either in January or February on the first few days of the first moon of the lunar new year. Apartments, offices and public buildings are decorated with auspicious orange trees, peach blossom and traditional calligraphy signifying happiness, prosperity and longevity. *Lai see*, red envelopes containing 'lucky' money, are handed out to children and single, young adults and accompanied by the expression, "Respectfully hope you get rich".

Ching Ming in April is the traditional occasion for sweeping and redecorating ancestral graves, many of which can be seen on the hillsides of the New Territories and Outlying Islands. The Dragon Boat Festival is celebrated in early summer, on the fifth day of the fifth moon. Remembering Qu Yuan, the ancient Chinese poet who committed suicide more than 2,300 years ago by jumping into a river, Tuen Ng indicates the beginning of summer, and the start of the new swimming season.

Possibly Hong Kong's most beautiful festival, the Mid-Autumn Festival, falls on the fifteenth day of the eighth moon, and gifts of mooncakes, fruit and wine are traditionally exchanged. Both adults and children carry lanterns to parks, beaches and the countryside to eat nighttime picnics and gaze at the beauty of the moon. The Chung Yung Festival, on the ninth day of the ninth moon, is another occasion for visiting ancestral graves, though many Hong Kong people also celebrate the festival by climbing hills in remembrance of an ancient Chinese family which fled to a mountain top to escape plague and death.

From the selection of an auspicious day for marriage to the choice of a child's name, unwritten spiritual laws of geomancy, or *feng shui*, govern almost every aspect of life in Hong Kong. The doors at the front entrance of the Mandarin Oriental on Connaught Road are said to have been placed at a certain angle, as were the escalators of the Hongkong Bank headquarters, to bar the way to ill-tempered ghosts.

Meaning literally 'wind and water', *feng shui* is normally used in the construction of buildings to facilitate harmony and bring good fortune to their inhabitants. The *feng shui* consultant, an extremely lucrative profession in construction-driven Hong Kong, assesses the site and recommends how to achieve balance between man and nature, location with colour and proportion. *Feng shui* is directly responsible for the preponderance of great fish tanks in Hong Kong offices.

The 12th-century magician-poet Bai Yue-shan incredibly predicted a city in the area of Hong Kong lit 'with a host of stars in the deep night, and ten thousand ships passing to and fro within the harbour.' He couldn't have been more accurate. Hong Kong bombards the senses: the skyward city soars spectacularly in breathtaking proximity; not far away the sea kisses golden beaches and undulating, green hills; incense burns outside designer label fashion boutiques; the cacophony of people, trams, buses, bicycles and motorcars crowds ceaselessly on to the streets; the neon-flooded harbour is crisscrossed by a timeless parade of ferries, *sampans*, *walla-wallas* and cargo vessels. Incredible to think it could ever have been any different.

Right and left
Hong Kong's fishing industry is dominated by the so-called 'boat people' who often spend their entire lives on junks clumped together in congested typhoon shelters. Last year, sea-going boat people landed over 180,000 tonnes of marine fish, most of it for local consumption. There are some 4,400 fishing vessels operating in Hong Kong, from state-of-the-art trawlers equipped with sonar to small wooden vessels with nothing more than an outboard motor and a net.

Below
Commercial towers, factories and major housing developments now dominate the skyline of Aberdeen which was once a quiet fishing village. However, Aberdeen's busy typhoon shelter is still home to some boat-dwellers who reach their floating abodes via tiny sampans.

Hong Kong has long been one of the world's busiest ports and it has become even busier in recent years as mainland China has started doing business with the rest of the world. The vast container yards of Hong Kong International Terminals, located in Kwai Chung, are an incredible sight, stacked high with colourful TEUs destined to be shipped all over the world.

Top
A United Airlines aircraft touches down at Hong Kong International Airport, Chek Lap Kok.

Middle left
A striking feature of the new airport's passenger terminal is a feeling of light and spaciousness.

Middle right
Almost a city in its own right, the airport passenger terminal meets the visitor's every need. In the weeks after its opening, the building was crowded with sightseers who came to marvel.

Bottom
The passenger terminal at Chek Lap Kok, designed by Sir Norman Foster, is the largest covered structure in the world. Covering an area of 49,000 square metres, it is 1.2 kilometres long and can handle 35 million passengers and three million tonnes of cargo a year.

Top
The brand new Hong Kong International Airport at Chek Lap Kok is the culmination of one of the world's largest infrastructure construction projects. Created from reclaimed land around one small island, the immense cost was a necessary price to pay to replace the overburdened Kai Tak, though many have questioned the cost to the environment and marine wildlife. It originally opened in 1998 with one 3,800-metre runway with the second runway becoming operational in May 1999. The new town of Tung Chung can be seen in the distance; built to support the airport, it was just a tiny fishing village a few years ago.

Above
Cathay Pacific is Hong Kong's main local airline serving regional and international destinations, and one of approximately 60 different airlines that fly into Hong Kong. About 650 aircraft take off and land in Hong Kong every day.

Right
Against a sunset backdrop, a plane makes its descent into Chek Lap Kok airport.

Above
The setting sun is reflected in the buildings of Wanchai and Central districts. Wanchai was notorious for its girlie bars during the 60s and 70s, and especially famous as the home of the fictitious Suzie Wong, but has undergone a renaissance in recent years. The Convention and Exhibition Centre extends into Victoria Harbour on the left. It was hurriedly completed in time to house the handover ceremony on 1st July, 1997, when Hong Kong was officially returned to Chinese sovereignty.
Two monuments now stand outside the building to commemorate this event: (left) a golden representation of the bauhinia flower—Hong Kong's official flower which is the emblem featured on the flag of the Special Administrative Region; and the Reunification Monument (opposite left).

Opposite right
Members of the Hong Kong Police conduct the flag-raising ceremony each morning beside the Reunification Monument.

Above
The many facets of Victoria Harbour. At night (above and right) the thousands of lights from the city buildings shine like so many jewels above the tranquil waters of the harbour as a cruise ship sails past and a Star Ferry plies its way back and forth. By day (left), increased activity in the harbour reflects on Hong Kong's status as one of the world's busiest ports.

Left
Looking down from the Peak, this view takes in Exchange Square in Central and, over the water, Tsim Sha Tsui with the Ocean Terminal and Gateway complex on the left. These towers are one of the many new construction projects on the Kowloon peninsula, following the closure of Kai Tak airport and the lifting of the height restrictions.

Right
The Star Ferry terminal in Tsim Sha Tsui on the left leads the eye to the twinkling lights of the buildings massed on the north shore of the island. The coloured lines leading away from the terminal show the route that the Star Ferries take across the harbour.

Above
Hong Kong's famous Victoria Harbour sees much boat traffic. The Star Ferry plies back and forth from Hong Kong island to Kowloon all day, while much larger cruise liners can dock at Ocean Terminal (above) and disembark their passengers directly into the shopping malls of Tsim Sha Tsui.

Left
The Peninsula Hong Kong is one of the city's most glamorous and much-loved hotels. Built in 1928, the legendary "Grande Dame of the Far East" is famous for its fleet of Rolls-Royces and for its elegant 1920s-style lobby where it is fashionable to take afternoon tea to the accompanying strains of a string quartet. The hotel was extensively renovated in 1994 when the tower behind was added.

Right
The Kowloon clock tower on the Tsim Sha Tsui waterfront is all that remains of the original Kowloon–Canton Railway Terminus building which was built in 1916. Behind is the ultra-modern Cultural Centre, Hong Kong's premier performing-arts centre.

Opposite Page
With a crowd so thick as to obscure most of the goods being sold in this open-air market, it is easy to understand why some parts of Hong Kong are purported to have the highest population density ever experienced by mankind. In the Mongkok district of Kowloon, more than 165,000 people are crammed on to each square kilometre.

Above
Early morning sun glints off the windows of Wanchai. Central Plaza towers above the Convention and Exhibition Centre.

Previous page
East meets West in no uncertain terms during the Dragon Boat Festival. Junks embellished with flags and dragon heads carry on a centuries-old tradition while the high-tech heights of Tsim Sha Tsui in the background are a vigorous reminder of the present.

Many New Territories farms devote their fields to the production of symbolic flower and fruit crops that decorate Hong Kong homes and offices during the major Chinese festivals. While the city is one of the world's most modern, traditional customs and beliefs are still deeply-rooted among the majority of its people.

Above
The manufacture of paper offerings is big business in Hong Kong. Designed to resemble expensive consumer goods—and even credit cards—offerings such as these are burned during funerals and festivals throughout the year to ensure that the dearly departed are well-heeled in the afterlife.

These sacks of rice (top) are destined for bins like the ones above or for direct consumption in restaurants. Rice is such an important staple that its various forms have different words: plain rice is mai; *cooked rice is* faan; *rice porridge is* juk; *and unhusked rice is* guk.

Above
Whether on Hong Kong's super-modern streets where fast-food joints and convenience stores proliferate or here on a back street where tradition still flourishes, it is a society constantly in motion. Shops such as this one arrange bowls of tea for quick draining, and even the moments taken to read a newspaper seem stolen from somewhere else. Many in Hong Kong have two or even three jobs with only one weekly rest day.

Left
T-shirt sellers do a roaring trade. During the handover to Chinese sovereignty in 1997, most focused on the transition, and, like the one in the girl's hand, the main ideas centred around the Chinese flag replacing the Union Jack.

Above

Besides dispensing medicinal teas, Hong Kong's hundreds of herbalists sell traditional remedies for all kinds of ills. Prepared while you wait, cures range from relatively innocuous sounding dried red dates for gastric disorders to exotica such as ground deer antler and dried sea horse. Many bizarre ingredients such as rhinoceros horn and tiger bones are now strictly illegal.

Left

There are flower stalls everywhere in Hong Kong and, as in the West, flowers are popular expressions of love. On Valentine's Day, however, prices go through the roof with a single red rose costing as much as HK$150.

Literally meaning 'little heart', dim sum features bite-sized morsels on small plates. To the right is siu mai, a steamed dumpling made of minced pork and shrimp.

Dim sum includes both sweet and savoury delicacies such as daan tats, hot custard tarts.

Most dim sum, such as steamed rolls with sweet filling (right), are served in small bamboo steamers.

Above
Another fast disappearing facet of old Hong Kong life. Bird aficionados frequently take their pet songbirds for a walk, but no longer can they go for yum cha in tea shops such as this one. Yum cha is the Chinese version of a tea break, featuring various kinds of snack called dim sum (left).

Right
At least one bird in a handmade cage is a common sight in many Chinese households. The centre for this hobby is a small alley in Kowloon nicknamed 'Bird Street'. Here dozens of dealers sell not just birds, but live grasshoppers and fresh larvae to feed them.

Far right
Indulging in a bit of dim sum is rarely a serene affair. Many dim sum restaurants span several floors and during peak times are packed with hundreds of diners all screaming and gesturing for their orders. Dim sum is served from trolley carts pushed through the aisles by serving girls who augment the hullabaloo by chanting traditional rhymes about the food.

The annual Rugby Sevens tournament is Hong Kong's biggest international sporting event and one of the most exciting competitions you will see anywhere. This abbreviated form of rugby is faster than the 15-a-side version of the game and the Rugby Sevens attracts top players from around the world.

The crowd really get into the spirit of the occasion by dressing up in outlandish outfits and singing, dancing, drinking and shouting themselves hoarse. The only question-mark over the whole tournament is: Who has the most fun – the players or the crowd?

Hong Kong people spend more than any other nation betting on horses. With two international class racing tracks at Happy Valley and Shatin (pictured), and countless Hong Kong Jockey Club outlets across the city where bets are placed, the amounts lodged on ordinary races are huge by world standards.

Far left, bottom
An echo of old empire; the Gurkha regiment band serenades the crowd during a Ladies' Day meeting at Shatin before the Handover.

47

Above
Seven hundred and fifty metres above sea level and surrounded by mountains, Po Lin Monastery on Lantau Island has about the best location of any of Hong Kong's 360-odd temples and monasteries. Visitors to the monastery can stay overnight in a dormitory— if they can get into the spirit of monastic living and endure the spartan comforts of an extremely hard bed.

Left and above
The world's largest scated, outdoor bronze Buddha is located at the Po Lin Monastery. The 24-metre giant (Tian Tan) statue sits on a lotus throne on top of a three-platform altar and weighs 202 tonnes. There are 268 steps to climb to reach it.

Above
Worshippers light joss-sticks at one of the SAR's many temples dedicated to Tin Hau, the Goddess of Heaven. Tin Hau is the patron saint of fishing folk—and anyone who comes near the sea including swimmers, surfers and sailors. It is Tin Hau who calms the waters, ensures that the day's catch is bountiful and keeps boats safe from harm.

Right
A priest beats a gong in the Temple of Ten Thousand Buddhas in Shatin, reached by a stiff 500-step climb through pine and bamboo groves. Besides boasting not just ten thousand Buddhas but 12,800, the monastery is home to a nine-storey pink pagoda and a mummified priest embalmed in gold leaf. This priest was the monastery's founder who died in 1965, and according to his wishes, was embalmed in a sitting position.

Left
Sunset over the outlying islands reveals the timeless, peaceful side of Hong Kong, away from the disturbances of the city.

Left
Dressed in a standard red ceremonial robe embellished with the symbols of Yin and Yang, a Taoist priest communes with the gods. It is only after he has put on his ceremonial head covering—the Tung Tin Long Mo—*that the gods will hear his prayers.*

Above
Immense incense coils hang from the ceiling of the Kwun Yum temple in Tai Hang, Causeway Bay. Each coil carries a red tag inscribed with the prayers and names of the worshippers who purchase them. The coils represent a 'long term' offering as they can burn for up to two weeks. The ceiling of this very beautiful little temple boasts a very dramatic and colourful design of a dragon.

Left
Even Hong Kong's powerful business tycoons have their spiritual side. Li Ka Shing, whose Cheung Kong and Hutchison Whampoa companies make him one of the city's leading entrepreneurs, built this temple in memory his wife.

Above
Celebrating Ta Chiu, the Taoist festival of peace and renewal, in Yuen Long, New Territories. Ta Chiu festivals are held, according to divination, at different times throughout the New Territories; sometimes at an interval of only three years, sometimes as long as 60. The spiritual objectives of Ta Chiu are still considered so important that hundreds of emigrants from overseas return to participate.

Below
Another spectacular celebration of the Ta Chiu festival takes place on the tiny island of Tap Mun Chau, off the coast of Sai Kung in the northeast New Territories. Here the lion dancers sent as tribute from neighbouring islands are welcomed by the village elders in their ceremonial robes.

Right
Placating the ghosts may be the serious purpose behind this parade staged during the Cheung Chau Bun Festival, but even the most ardent of believers can't keep a straight face all the time. This festival features 60-foot high towers of edible pink and white buns offered first to the ghosts, and later to the living.

Rowing teams of 20 or even 40 compete in races held throughout the SAR in June during the Dragon Boat Festival. Each boat is festooned with a detachable dragon head and tail. As part of the racing ritual, the eyes of each head are dotted with a mixture of red paint and chicken blood to imbue them with a 'live' force. The races are to commemorate an ancient court scholar who committed suicide by hurling himself into a river in protest against the corruption of government officials.

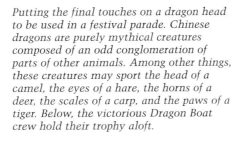

Putting the final touches on a dragon head to be used in a festival parade. Chinese dragons are purely mythical creatures composed of an odd conglomeration of parts of other animals. Among other things, these creatures may sport the head of a camel, the eyes of a hare, the horns of a deer, the scales of a carp, and the paws of a tiger. Below, the victorious Dragon Boat crew hold their trophy aloft.

Details of the innumerable festivals honouring ghosts or gods staged every year in the SAR. As Hong Kong has prospered, festivities have become more elaborate. The 'flower board', right, with its messages of peace and purification was part of a massive Ta Chiu festival costing hundreds of thousands of dollars and shared by many villages.

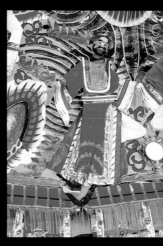

The spectacularly beautiful southern coastline of Lamma Island—remote and almost deserted apart from a handful of houses in the two small villages of Yung Shue Ha and Tung O, just visible on the shore of Tung O Bay in the centre of the photograph. Archaeologists have discovered some of Hong Kong's oldest settlements in this area, unearthing remains dating back to 4000 BC.

Above
The 'Produce Green Organic Farm' near Loi Tung was established by a foundation to help preserve traditional, chemical-free, methods of farming. Part of the land is farmed by enthusiasts, and the rest is leased to full-time farmers who raise produce to sell to the 35,000 visitors who pass through each year. The rice paddy here is almost the last in the territory.

Left
A traditional New Territories village stands in the security of the hills. Apart from the inevitable incursions of the modern era, life goes on here much as it always has in rural Hong Kong.

Right
Except for the cellophane and the higher price tag of the vegetables (bottom right), all of these pictures show a traditional way of living that still endures. Thousand-year old eggs (top right) have long been a delicacy; farmers have long watered their crops by hand; and pickled radishes (centre right) have long been dried in the sun in baskets such as these. The smiling lady on the right is collecting vegetables at Ta Kwu Ling on the China border. Grown without heavy use of chemicals they command a higher price than those imported from China itself and often go straight to the tables of Hong Kong's top hotels and restaurants.

Spectacularly situated on a high promontory between Aberdeen and Deep Water Bay, 87-hectare Ocean Park is Hong Kong's premier park for recreation, boasting Southeast Asia's largest oceanarium. Over 40 million people have visited the park since it was originally opened with Hong Kong Jockey Club funding in 1977. Besides entertainment, Ocean Park also has a more serious role: in 1996 the Ocean Park Conservation Foundation was set up to coordinate regional efforts in the conservation of endangered whales and dolphins. Access to the headland is either by the world's longest outdoor escalator, seen here snaking up the hillside, or by cable car from the other side of the hill.

Cheung Chau (meaning "long island" in Cantonese) island is just a 40-minute ferry ride from Hong Kong and a popular weekend destination. The tiny island is just 2.5 square kilometres and used to be populated by pirates. Nowadays, fishing junks still crowd the typhoon shelter and it's a great place to go for a fresh seafood dinner.

Opposite page
The towers of the Tsing Ma Bridge point the way to the new Hong Kong International Airport in the distance at Chek Lap Kok.

Above
The Tsing Ma Bridge (centre of photograph) meets the elegant Ting Kau Bridge (on the left), which connects Tsing Yi Island with the northwest New Territories and is at the southern end of a new express road system that not only connects the whole of Hong Kong to its international airport on Lantau Island, but also carries traffic directly into southern China.

Below
Sunset silhouettes the graceful lines of the world's longest combined road and rail suspension bridge at 2.2 kilometres. The main span of the Tsing Ma Bridge is 1,377 metres long, incorporating 160,000 kilometres of suspension cable—enough to circle the world four times.

Posters advertising various performances by the Hing Fung Ming Cantonese Opera Troupe, one of the most popular and highly acclaimed in Hong Kong.

The lead actor of the Hing Fung Ming troupe, Mr Lam Kam Tong (right), carefully prepares his make-up for another performance. He has been performing opera in Hong Kong for over 40 years. (above) Mr Lam in action in a scene from the opera "A Blood Oath Sworn at the Grotto", and (top) with lead actress Ms Mui Suet Sze in "The Reincarnation of the Peach Blossom".

Traditional Chinese gentlemen have always taken their songbirds in their cages for a walk in the morning. Nowadays, the cages are just as likely to decorate the insides of homes, and are often sold at street-side stalls which specialise in them. Vast shopping centres like Times Square in Causeway Bay are home to innumerable retail outlets with designer label goods and restaurants with cuisines from all over the world. Dried, preserved and pressed meat, particularly sausage and duck, are popular local delicacies sold at the main food markets located in most areas.

Silk imported from China is both beautiful and expensive, but it is still one of the best bargain buys. Lengths of material bought may be taken to any of Hong Kong's 4,000 tailors for custom-made tailoring—another of the city's traditional attractions. Hong Kong's own textile industry produces mainly cotton, most of which is purchased by local clothing manufacturers.

Left
Strong local traditions in the performing arts lead many children to train. Young ballerinas at some of the leading schools often dance at the opening of important sporting or cultural occasions.

Left
Hong Kong's famous fleet of colourful trams affords an ideal way for tourists to view the street-life of Hong Kong Island. The city's first mass public transport system began in 1904 and still offers one of the most economical and environmentally friendly modes of transport for its residents. Carrying around 337,000 people each day, the trams provide a dramatic contrast to the usually frenetic pace of life in this city.

Above
Jumbo is the largest of three floating restaurants located in Aberdeen harbour, home to the SAR's largest community of boat people. The three-storey restaurant is reached by sampan and affords a glimpse of the crowded typhoon shelter. Aberdeen's natural harbour once served as an anchorage for early voyagers to China long before the British arrived.

Right
When the sun goes down, the lights come on in Hong Kong. Everything from product advertisements to restaurants, pawn-shop logos to short-time hotels vie for attention.

Above
Picturesque as this quiet harbour with its fishing boats may be, it is likely that the traditional fishing life of Hong Kong's boat people is drawing to a close. Though the amount of fish caught has continued to escalate, the number of working boat people has decreased. As fishing vessels become diesel-powered and thus more expensive to operate and to own, poorer fishing families are driven to shore.

Opposite Page
Fishing off the Sai Kung Peninsula.

Right
Boats of all sizes arrive packed with fishing folk and sightseers to witness the annual Tap Mun Chau festival. This normally quiet, now sparsely populated island comes alive with this colourful and dramatic event.

Following Pages (pages 78-79)
What must surely be one of the most dramatic night views in the world—from the Peak, on Hong Kong Island. Each year, there are new and ever more spectacular additions to the cityscape.

Following page (page 80)
Little stands in the way of progress in Hong Kong. The venerable Hilton Hotel, for many years an institution in this city, was demolished to make way for the Cheung Kong Center, which now competes for attention with the Bank of China (left) and the Hong Kong and Shanghai Bank (right).

77

AN A TO Z OF HONG KONG

A

Aberdeen Hong Kong's oldest settlement was once home to a 50,000-strong fishing community, but a government re-housing scheme has reduced the numbers to a few hundred. Nevertheless, exploration of the remaining fishing boats and the floating restaurants is a fascinating experience by sampan, which can be found by the main seawall opposite Aberdeen Centre.

Antiques Central's Hollywood Road is the main area for antiques, arts and crafts, although the large China Products stores and small curio shops in places like Ocean Terminal and the Silk Road arcade in the adjoining Omni Hongkong Hotel are also worth visiting. Neolithic pots, Qing cloisonne and Imperial embroideries, Burmese puppets, Indian brassware and Thai buddhas are just a sample of the vast range available. Beware of 'authentic fakes'.

B

Beaches Considering the poor water quality at most of Hong Kong's 42 beaches, it is surprising that swimming is the city's most popular summer recreation. Repulse Bay with close-by shops and restaurants probably attracts the most people with the less-crowded and cleanest ones being located on the Outlying Islands and in the New Territories.

Beverages What to drink with Chinese food is a difficult question to answer. At important banquets many Hong Kong people prefer VSOP or XO cognac, although the Mainland's Tsingtao beer or local San Miguel and Carlsberg are more commonly consumed at regular meals. Chinese wines such as *mao tai*, *kao liang* and *siu hing* have an extremely high alcoholic content. Chinese tea, however, without milk or sugar, is probably the best accompaniment and enjoyed at all Chinese restaurants.

Bird Market Songbirds have long been prized in China, remaining a favourite pet in traditional Hong Kong households. In Mong Kok's Bird Garden in Yuen Po Street, hundreds of birds are on sale, at prices which often reveal that the birds' singing abilities are valued more than the colourfulness of their plumage. The market is located off Prince Edward Road West, near the Flower Market, not far from Prince Edward MTR station.

C

Causeway Bay One of Hong Kong's busiest shopping and entertainment districts, Causeway Bay boasts numerous Japanese department stores as well as Times Square, one of the city's most modern shopping malls. Vogue Alley, Jardine's Bazaar and Jardine's Crescent are better for bargains. The Noon Day Gun in front of the Excelsior Hotel, Tin Hau Temple, Victoria Park are the major attractions.

Climate Subtropical Hong Kong stands just south of the Tropic of Cancer with a typhoon season from July to September. In spring, from March to mid-May, the average temperature ranges from 18–27°C. In summer, June to September, temperatures reach as high as 34°C with 90% plus humidity. The best time to visit is autumn, September to December, when temperatures drop to a pleasant 18–28°C. Winter from December to February is coolish, 14–20°C, but fog and rain are common.

Culture In recent years, Hong Kong has developed a well-earned reputation as a major centre for the performing arts. The main venues include City Hall, Cultural Centre, Arts Centre, Academy for the Performing Arts, with frequent performances of opera, Western and Chinese classical music, modern and traditional dance and ballet by top international and local artists, including the city's world-class philharmonic and Chinese orchestras. Alternative venues like the Fringe Club offer more avant-garde productions. The month-long Hong Kong Arts Festival which takes place annually from February to March, is now an established event on the international arts calendar.

D

Dai Pai Dong These street-side food stalls are something of an acquired taste for visitors to Hong Kong. Locals are careful about cleanliness in such places, generally sterilising their chopsticks with hot tea before proceeding to eat. While most of these cheap eateries are unhygienic, they remain popular, serving everything from tripe to noodles quickly. On average, Hong Kong people take one meal every day in one kind of restaurant or another.

E

Eight Many Chinese, and Cantonese speakers in particular, hold strong beliefs in numerology—that certain numbers have particular symbolic significance. The number eight in Cantonese, for instance, is one of the most auspicious as it sounds similar to the word for wealth.

F

Feng Shui Translating as wind and water, *feng shui* is the ancient Chinese science of balancing the *yin* and *yang* (male and female) in the natural world. Experts known as geomancers play an important role in Hong Kong society, particularly in the business world, where they are called upon to recommend the best site for a building and its decoration and furnishing. Offices facing water are especially auspicious, those that do not need to redress the balance. It is no surprise that aquariums are enormously popular in Hong Kong.

Fanling Lying in the heart of the New Territories, the area has been extensively settled for many centuries and now contains a major new town and nature reserves. The renowned Royal Hong Kong Golf Club is also located there with some of Asia's oldest links. The course and clubhouse are open to visitors on weekdays, but not on weekends or public holidays. To play, advance telephone bookings are recommended. The club is just a five-minute taxi ride from Fanling KCR station.

G

Golden Mile Formerly known as Nathan's Folly, today's neon-covered Nathan Road is full of glittering hotels, restaurants and shopping centres like the Park Lane Boulevard. Built on the orders of Governor Nathan, a military engineer, Kowloon's main thoroughfare originally failed to attract many settlers and buildings, most probably because of its proximity to the borderland of Boundary Street.

Government House Built in 1855 in Upper Albert Road, it was home to the British governors, but now plays a purely ceremonial role. One of the few colonial-style buildings still remaining, it was extensively restored and modified by the Japanese during the occupation of Hong Kong in the Second World War.

H

Happy Valley Between Wan Chai and Causeway Bay is Hong Kong's oldest horse-racing venue. The first races were held here in 1846 on land reclaimed from a disease-ridden swamp. Happy Valley trams run right next to the course. Meetings are held there every Wednesday evening during the September–June season.

Hungry Ghosts Festival Yue Lan normally takes place on the 15th day of the Seventh Moon which usually falls in September. The festival placates those spirits that have become dispossessed, and who return to wreak havoc in the material world. Offerings are made in the form of paper replicas of material possessions such as cars, houses, food and money. The replicas are burnt, allowing the disgruntled ghosts to return satisfied with their new-found wealth.

I

IIs Despite extensive border security and patrols, illegal immigrants (IIs) still manage to enter Hong Kong. Highly-paid work is the major attraction, as Hong Kong has one of the world's highest standards of living. Many are caught during spot checks on the streets, in MTR stations and on building sites, where large numbers find work. Hong Kong authorities have the legal right to stop anyone and ask that they produce their identity card or travel document.

J

Jade Market Supporting 450 registered stall-holders, visitors are advised not to buy top-grade jade here unless they are experts. In Chinese culture, jade has substantial spiritual value and when carved into certain figures it represents wealth (deer), good fortune (tiger) and power (dragon). Jordan MTR station is closest to its location on the junction of Kansu and Battery streets.

K

Kam Tin This walled village was the 10th-century settling place of the Tang clan, the first of the five great Cantonese clans to migrate to the New Territories. The current site was built during the 16th century as a defensive stronghold against tigers, rival clans and wandering bands of Ming dynasty followers who had turned to piracy and banditry. The number 51 bus service links Kam Tin to the Tsuen Wan Ferry, just south of the Tsuen Wan MTR station.

L

Lamma Island In the main village, Yung Shue Wan, old China mixes with the modern West. Modern boutiques stand next to traditional Chinese stores, Western restaurants next to noodle shops. The village has a Mediterranean feel, reinforced by the hordes of holidaymakers who crowd the ferries and holiday flats every weekend. A regular ferry service leaves from pier 5 in Central.

Lok Ma Chau This lookout point is Hong Kong's best view of China, and in particular the remarkable skyline of the Shenzhen Economic Zone. The 68M bus from Tsuen Wan MTR station will take you there.

M

Mai Po Marshes The most important site for nature preservation in Hong Kong, Mai Po is a restricted area, managed by the Worldwide Fund for Nature. Its 380 hectares of mudflats, shrimp ponds and mangrove swamps are home to more than 250 types of birds and it is a significant international site for migratory species. Situated in the border area, Mai Po is under increasing pressure from encroaching developers in both China and Hong Kong. Fears persist about its future.

Middle Kingdom Located next to Ocean Park, Southeast Asia's largest entertainment and leisure centre, this is a 'living history of Chinese culture'. Re-telling the stories of 13 dynasties and 5,000 years of history, the Middle Kingdom also features arts and crafts demonstrations, live theatre and cultural shows. A special Citybus leaves Admiralty MTR station every half an hour for Ocean Park and the Middle Kingdom.

N

Noon Day Gun Fired every day at the stroke of midday, and other special occasions like the stroke of midnight on New Year's Eve, the gun has even been immortalised in song. According to Noel Coward: 'In Hong Kong they strike a gong and fire off a noon day gun. But mad dogs and Englishmen go out in the midday sun.' Located in a small garden opposite the Excelsior hotel, accessible via a tunnel under Gloucester Road, the gun is within easy walking distance of the Causeway Bay MTR station.

O

Opera Traditional Beijing, Cantonese and Chiu Chow operas and musical dramas with their elaborate make-up, costumes and lyrics are occasionally recreated at selected venues. Over the years, it has often been used as a medium for criticism of officialdom, though its general appeal lies in its representation of archetypal characters and qualities such as virtue, corruption, youth, age, violence and lust.

P

Peak Tram Once the only way up Victoria Peak apart from walking, this funicular railway is a must for every visitor. Trams run every 10–15 minutes every day and take about eight minutes to climb the 373 metres to one of the world's most spectacular views, shops and restaurants. The lower terminus is on Garden Road and can be reached by bus from Star Ferry, next to City Hall in Central.

Q

Qigong The ancient Chinese breathing exercise that has enjoyed a resurgence in recent years. Much research has been conducted into this psychic art, with many believing it to be a potential cure for cancer and many other ailments.

Queen's Road West This area has become famous for its sights, sounds and smells. Shops on either side spill over with cheongsam wedding dresses, salted fish and dried squid, coloured paper lanterns, Chinese herbs and bamboo dim sum baskets.

R

Religion Most religions of the world are to be found in Hong Kong and are currently practised with complete freedom. Many faiths offer services in English—check in local newspapers for details. Significant numbers of local people are adherents of various Christian denominations. However, the large majority worship both Taoist and Buddhist deities, as well as ancestral spirits.

S

St John's Cathedral Believed to be the oldest Anglican church in Asia, it was inaugurated in 1849 and modelled after 13th-century early English and decorated Gothic designs. Located in a hillside grove of trees off Garden Road, Central, behind the Hongkong Bank headquarters on Queen's Road, it is one of Hong Kong's longest standing colonial buildings.

Snake Soup Served with chrysanthemum flowers, snake soup is a heart-warming winter dish much loved by Hong Kong people. The snake's gall bladder can also be removed and added to a glass of wine as a cure for arthritis or as a general stimulant.

T

Tai Chi Traditional Chinese shadow boxing is a series of more than 200 individual movements flowing into one motion that aims to exercise every muscle in the body. The best places to watch devotees practise are in Causeway Bay's Victoria Park and the Botanical Gardens in Central between about 6–8am.

Ten Thousand Buddhas Monastery There are actually 12,800 images of Buddha at this major attraction in Sha Tin. Each one is equal in size but has a slightly different pose. Five hundred steps lead up to the temple that was founded by the monk Yuet Kai. Embalmed in gold leaf, his body is on display in a glass case, and is believed to have been supernaturally preserved after death. The monastery is signposted from Sha Tin KCR station.

U

University Museum The oldest museum in Hong Kong, its prized possession is a collection of bronzeware from the Yuan dynasty (AD1276–1368), the largest of its kind in the world. Artefacts from the Warring States Period and the Tang and Qing dynasties are also on display. Located on Bonham Road in Mid-Levels, the University is served by bus number 3 which departs from outside Jardine House in Central.

V

Victoria Peak There are several walking routes which encircle the Peak, as well as a country park access point. Offering 360 degrees of spectacular views of Hong Kong, this is probably the city's premier tourist highlight, day or night. At one time the only way up was by sedan chair, although these days taxis, buses or the Peak Tram are usually preferred. It is, however, possible to walk up the 554 metres to the top.

W

Walla-walla The origin of the names of these motorised sampans which ceaselessly cross the harbour is unknown. Some say it's the sound that they make, while others suggest it is the name of the first of its kind owned by a man from Wala Wala, Washington, USA.

Wong Tai Sin Temple Bearing the name of Hong Kong's most popular Taoist deity, this temple plays host to more than three million visitors every year. Its red pillars, two-tiered golden roof, yellow lattice-work and multi-coloured carvings provide a startling contrast to the surrounding local government housing estates. The temple is a three-minute walk north of Wong Tai Sin MTR station.

Y

Yue People Possibly Hong Kong's first inhabitants, little is known about these pre-historic, maritime people who lived on China's south-eastern seaboard. Sometimes referred to as the Hundred Yue.

Z

Zoological and Botanical Gardens Established in 1864 with archetypal Victorian features including a wrought-iron bandstand, the gardens are home to many exotic birds, mammals, flora and fauna. The flamingos are an extremely popular attraction. The red-cheeked gibbon collection is the world's largest. Access is from Garden Road in Central.